PUFFIN BOOKS

The Monster School Curric...

Are you ghoulishly wicked and reve... ...horrible enough to be a star pupil of Monster School? If you want to be a mega monster – to terrify your friends, drive your teachers crazy and generally create chaos wherever you go – then this is the book for you.

Learn how to make Maggots in Chocolate Sauce at Spookery class, play games like Screamin' Demon at Party Studies, and totally confuse your teacher in Mammothematics. With hilarious monster jokes and tips, advice on how to be breathtakingly ugly, a monster movie guide, even a problem page for all those worried werewolves and vampires, you're sure to have a monster of a good read!

Martyn Forrester was born in 1952 in Guernsey and has worked both as a teacher and as an advertising copywriter. Now a full-time writer, he lives with his family in Putney.

Martyn Forrester

The Monster School Curriculum

A step-by-step guide on how to be a complete monster

Illustrated by Ian Cunliffe

PUFFIN BOOKS

PUFFIN BOOKS

Published by the Penguin Group
Penguin Books Ltd, 27 Wrights Lane, London W8 5TZ, England
Penguin Books USA Inc., 375 Hudson Street, New York, New York 10014, USA
Penguin Books Australia Ltd, Ringwood, Victoria, Australia
Penguin Books Canada Ltd, 10 Alcorn Avenue, Toronto, Ontario, Canada M4V 3B2
Penguin Books (NZ) Ltd, 182–190 Wairau Road, Auckland 10, New Zealand

Penguin Books Ltd, Registered Offices: Harmondsworth, Middlesex, England

First published 1993
10 9 8 7 6 5 4 3 2 1

Text copyright © Martyn Forrester, 1993
Illustrations copyright © Ian Cunliffe, 1993
All rights reserved

The moral right of the author has been asserted

Typeset by Datix International Limited, Bungay, Suffolk
Set in 12/14 Monophoto Times
Printed in England by Clays Ltd, St Ives plc

How to Become a Mega Monster

Step 1

Buy **The Monster School Curriculum.**

Step 2

Read it.

This Copy of *The Monster School Curriculum* Belongs to:

Monster's Name ....

Monster's Address

Cave name or number..

Town or city ....

Postcode ....

Telephone number ....

Age (in human years)..

Age (in monster years) ....

Date of birth or manufacture...

Height when standing ....

Height when lying down ....

Colour of hair ....

Colour of eyes..

Colour of nose ....

Number of noses..

Any distinguishing features? ....

Any normal features?..

My boyfriend/girlfriend is ....

who

☐ is as sweet as sugar (and twice as lumpy)

☐ has a heart of gold (yellow and hard)

☐ has the complexion of a peach (orange and fuzzy)

☐ has a very soft heart (and a head to match)

Introduction

Monsters aren't born that way, you know. They don't just come into the world automatically knowing how to terrify their teachers, pester their sisters, wind up their brothers, drive their parents crazy and generally create chaos and disorder wherever they go.

No, they have to learn everything from scratch, and in the case of some monsters that means quite a lot of scratching.

No wonder the Monster School has such a busy curriculum!

As you know, a school is not a school if it doesn't have rules, and the Monster School is no exception. The only difference is that MONSTER RULES are sensible rules, because they guarantee that being a monster is brilliant fun:

1. **Don't be a monster** unless it's fun for everyone involved – always pick on someone your own size, or preferably bigger.

2. **Never be a monster** with someone who is old, disabled, nervous or shy.

3. **Never be a monster** in front of the Queen: always let her go first.

4. **Never be a monster** if it's going to hurt someone's feelings.

5. **Never be a monster** if it's going to make someone cry.

6. **Never be a monster** if it's going to make someone cross.

7. In short, **never be a monster** if it's going to spoil someone's day, cause loss of life or limb, or trigger off a total global thermonuclear war.

However:

1. **Do be a monster** with the school bully.

2. **Do be a monster** with your best friend.

3. **Do be a monster** with your brothers, your sisters, your sister's boyfriend and your parents – as long as you're wearing full protective body armour.

4. **Do be a monster** with your teacher – as long as you have no ambition to stay at school.

Monster School Entrance Exam

Just because you want to come to this school doesn't mean you're automatically allowed in. First, you have to prove that you have all the determination, knowledge and monster potential that it takes to be a star pupil. So to see if you, too, have what it takes to join the world's most exclusive educational establishment, just answer the following simple questions:

1. **Do you think Frankenstein's monster is:**
a. Possibly dead?
b. Almost certainly dead?
c. Absolutely, definitely, one hundred per cent dead handsome?

2. Do you think Zombies are:
a. The latest brand of street-hot footwear?
b. A team of bees from Zom?
c. The walking dead, their faces drained of blood and with eyes that have a terrifying stare and never blink?

3. Do you think Monster School is:
a. The wrong spelling of 'skool'?
b. The place you go to between waking up and watching *The Addams Family*?
c. The place that feeds and nurtures your brain so you can grow up dead educated and write mega-brill books like *The Monster School Curriculum*?

4. Which of the following sentences best describes your feelings at 8.30 on a Monday morning?

a. 'Hey, OK, guys – let's go learn a few things!'
b. 'Please God, let my teacher be ill today.'
c. 'Zzzzzzzzzzzzzzzzzz.'

How you score:

Mostly 'a's: Are you one sad, pathetic human or what! Put down this copy of *The Monster School Curriculum* and walk quietly away. There's nothing here for you, humanoid features.

Mostly 'b's: You're not a human, but you'd probably like to be one.

Mostly 'c's: Welcome to Monster School, ugly!!!

Monster School Staff

Head: Terry Fie
Deputy Head: Dee Monic
Absolutely No Head At All: The ghost of Anne Boleyn

Monster School Matron: Ann T. Septic
Monster School Nurse: Tommy Ache

Head of Computer and Brain Transplant Studies: Mike Rowe-Chip

Head of Biology and Deadly Amoeba Studies: M. Brio

Head of Metalwork and Advanced Robotics: Hal U. Minium.

Head of Monster Insect Studies: Amos Quito

Head of Frankenstein's Laboratory: Anna Tomical

Head of Earth Monster Studies: Abe Ominable

Head of Supernatural Studies: Eve L. Spirit

My Monster Class

The monster dunce ....

The monster swot ....

The monster clown ....

The monster bossy-boots ....

The monster giggler ....

The monster sports champ...

The best-dressed monster...

The worst-dressed monster ....

The monster tell-tale...

The monster bully...

The monster show-off...

The monster chatterbox...

The monster sulk ....

The latest arriving monster ....

The most forgetful monster ....

The tidiest monster ....

The untidiest monster ....

The monster monster (your name goes here!)

....

Anguish Language: Writing and Spelling

Teacher: Dick Shunry

Dick Shunry: Do you know a word with 26 letters in it?
Monster School pupil: Alphabet.

Dick Shunry: What play by William Shakespeare makes monsters cry?
Monster School pupil: Romeo and Ghouliet.

Dick Shunry: What word is always spelt incorrectly?
Monster School pupil: Incorrectly.

Dick Shunry: What is the longest word in the English language?
Monster School pupil: Smiles – because there's a mile between the first and last letters.

Dick Shunry: What is the second largest word in the English language?
Monster School pupil: Elastic – because it stretches.

Dick Shunry: Give me a sentence with the word 'fascinate' in it.
Monster School pupil: My little sister has a coat with ten buttons but she can only fasten eight.

Dick Shunry: Give me a sentence with the word 'gruesome' in it.
Monster School pupil: My mum wanted some flowers so my dad grew some.

Dick Shunry: What is the longest sentence you can think of?
Monster School pupil: Life imprisonment.

Dick Shunry: Give me a sentence with the word 'centimetre' in it.
Monster School pupil: My granny came to visit and I was sent to meet her.

• **MONSTER TIP**
Put up a notice that says 'Dry Paint' on a wall in the school corridor and watch for a while. You'll find that many people (including teachers) will actually touch the wall to make sure that it is dry!

If you want to be a really mega-wicked monster, it's no good going around saying wimpy puns like 'Fangs very much' or 'Best vicious of the season'. I mean, that's monster*ish*, but what you really need to practise is how to howl and roar and gnash your teeth. To get these essential monster skills spot-on, you need to attend the **Monster School Anguish Course** in

Monster Tongue Twisters

A very good start is:

Mummies munch much mush,
Monsters munch much mush,
Many mummies and monsters
Must munch much mush.

But if that's too much for you to get your fangs around, why not try:

The glum ghoul grows glummer.

When you've mastered that, have a go at:

Frankenstein favours five free fruit floats.

And if that's all very easy-peasy, gross and sleazy, then get yourself stuck into this little lot:

Freddy Phantom threw three free throws.

Faint phantoms fear fat flat flounders.

Sixty-six sticky skeletons.

The Abominable Snowman seeks six thick sticks.

'Six small slick seals,' the skeleton screamed.

The Swiss witch bewitched the thin twin tinsmith.

Which Swiss witch bewitched which witch's watch?

The flimsy phantom fled the flood-filled flat.

● MONSTER TIP

Here is a monstrous little trick to make your friends faint! This time, you're going to eat one of your fingers . . .

What you need is a piece of bread stick the same length as one of your fingers. Hold it in place by squeezing it between your second and third fingers and then, when it is time to make your announcement that you are going to eat one of your fingers, hold up your hand (only for a second or two, or your audience will notice that you have too many fingers!) and break off what appears to be your middle finger. Now munch away merrily and watch your audience go green.

Anguish Ow! Level

1. Which famous novelist wrote *Withering Bites* and lots of other books about dinosaurs and monsters?
a. Claudia Legoff
b. Terry Fie
c. Dee Monic
d. Charlotte Brontesaurus

2. Which of the following novels is by Thomas Hardy?
a. *Tess of the Dormobiles*
b. *Nightmare on Casterbridge Street*
c. *Fart from the Badly Behaved Crowd*

3. What is the name of the present Poet Laureate?
a. Nerys Hughes
b. Emlyn Hughes
c. Ted Hughes
d. Howard Hughes

4. How do you spell Shakespeare?

5. Which of the following greetings does not feature in a Shakespeare play?
a. 'What ho, Horatio.'
b. 'Holla, Barnardo!'
c. 'Peace, ho – Caesar speaks.'
d. 'Yo, bro, my main man – maximum respect!'

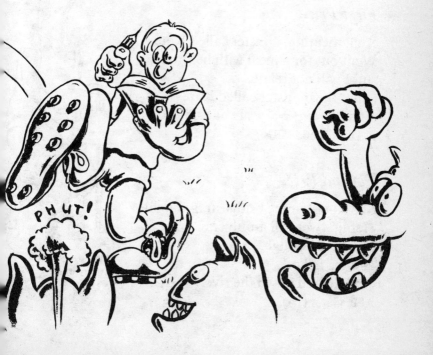

PHUT!

Monster School Poetry Competition

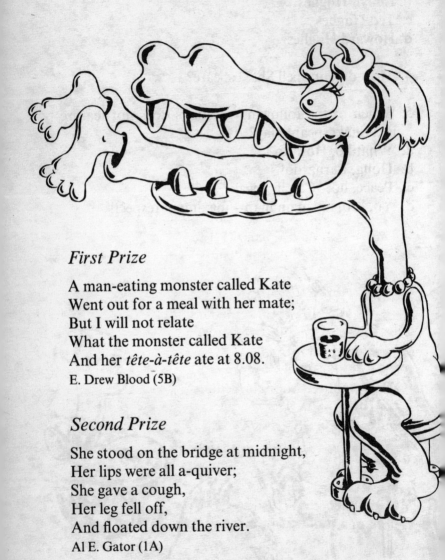

First Prize

A man-eating monster called Kate
Went out for a meal with her mate;
But I will not relate
What the monster called Kate
And her *tête-à-tête* ate at 8.08.

E. Drew Blood (5B)

Second Prize

She stood on the bridge at midnight,
Her lips were all a-quiver;
She gave a cough,
Her leg fell off,
And floated down the river.

Al E. Gator (1A)

Third Prize

A clever young monster called Sue
Could always find something to do;
When it bored her to go
On a walk to and fro,
She reversed it, and walked fro and to.

Dai A. Bolical (3C)

Runners Up

There once was a monster called Fred
Who used to eat onions in bed;
His mother said: 'Sonny,
It's not very funny,
Why don't you eat people instead?'

O. Fensiff (1C)

There was a young monster from Ealing,
Who boarded a plane for Darjeeling;
He saw on the door:
'Please don't spit on the floor.'
So he carefully spat on the ceiling.

Buster Kneecap (2A)

A ghostly young monster called Paul
Once went to a fancy dress ball;
To shock every guest,
He went there undressed,
But no one could see him at all.

Mandy Ceased (5A)

A sea monster saw a big tanker,
Bit a hole in her side and then sank her;
He swallowed the crew
In a minute or two,
And then picked his teeth with the anchor.

Philippa Bucket (3C)

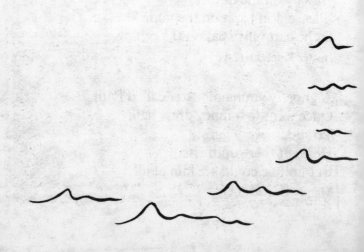

Monster School Library

Monster School Definitions

Blotting paper: something you look for while the ink dries

Coward: someone who wears water wings in the bath

Free speech: when you use someone else's telephone

Friend: someone who has the same enemies as you

Out of bounds: an exhausted kangaroo

Physics: the science of making lemonade and other fizzy drinks

School: a place where they teach you things you'll never need to know when you leave it

School desk: a wastepaper basket with a lid

Teacher: a person who is always late for school when you are early and early when you are late

Temper: something you can lose but still have

Tortoise: what our teacher did

Monster School Science Lesson

Teachers: Molly Kewl and Dinah Mite

Billy Bloggs is dead,
We won't see him no more;
For what he thought was H_2O
Was H_2SO_4.

Molly Kewl: Why is the sea so salty?
Monster School pupil: Because fish sweat a lot.

Dinah Mite: What is used as a conductor of electricity?
Monster School pupil: Why . . . er . . .
Dinah Mite: That's correct – wire. Now, can you tell me the name of a unit of electricity?
Monster School pupil: What?
Dinah Mite: Correct – it is the watt.

Molly Kewl: How did the Chinese discover gunpowder?
Monster School pupil: It came to them in a flash.

How to Look Beautifully Ugly

Do you have trouble with your looks?
Do boys rush up to you in the street and say, 'Gosh,
you're beautiful'?
Are you so unbelievably handsome that girls can't help
falling at your feet?

IF SO, DON'T WORRY! SOON YOU COULD
BE UGLIER THAN YOU EVER DREAMED
POSSIBLE, THANKS TO THESE AMAZING
HINTS AND TIPS FROM THE MONSTER
SCHOOL UGLY PARLOUR!

With our handy, up-to-date advice on how to look
breathtakingly ugly, you'll soon be winning ugly con-
tests left, right and centre and knocking them dead at
the Monster School disco . . .

☐ Cut out a small piece of black paper the same
size as a tooth, lick it, and stick it to one of your
front teeth. You'll look as if your tooth has been
knocked out.

☐ You can use nose putty (obtainable from theatri-
cal costumiers) to make a nice wart to stick on the
end of your nose. For added attractiveness, why not
add a few hairs plucked from a paintbrush?

☐ Nose putty can also be used to create a seductive
Frankenstein's monster type of forehead.

☐ Use black lipstick, not red, to make yourself look like Dracula.

☐ Make a Dracula cape by cutting black material into a semi-circle, with the straight edge about 150cm long. In the middle of the straight edge cut a small semi-circle for the back of your neck. Stitch some black ribbon to this edge so that you can tie the tape around your neck. Wear the cape with black trousers, white shirt and black bowtie.

☐ Practise a sinister laugh.

☐ Use red lipstick or face paint to put two puncture marks on your neck and a thin trickle of blood, to look as though you've been bitten by a vampire.

☐ Dracula-like teeth can be cut out of a sheet of shiny white card. When placed under your top lip they will look just like real fangs – especially if you paint the ends red to look as though you've been sucking blood.

☐ Make your own horror mask in *papier mâché* by pasting scraps of newspaper on to an inflated balloon and allowing it to dry. Cut the dried ball in half lengthwise and you will have the bases for two masks. For that special hairy monster look, cover the face with brown wool or string.

☐ Put a rolled-up towel around your shoulders before getting dressed. This will give you a nice

Quasimodo hunchback effect. If you really want to go to town, put a small pebble in your shoe to make you limp.

☐ Turn your hands into horror hands by using face paints to paint on blue veins, warts and scars.

☐ Make yourself look like a Zombie by combing your hair straight back off your face and covering your entire face and lips with talcum powder. Use grey eyeshadow to put dark rings around your eyes, and a little under your cheekbones to give yourself a thin, hollow look. Don't forget to draw a thin trickle of blood from your mouth.

☐ To give yourself a horrible-looking scar, put one teaspoon of gelatine powder in a cup, and add one drop of red food colouring and one teaspoonful of hot water. Stir very quickly with a spoon and as soon as the mixture is cool, stick the gunge on your cheek and push it around to make a lumpy, uneven surface. The mixture will stick to any part of your body and will look like a nasty burn. To remove it, simply peel it off.

☐ To make fake fingernails, cut pieces out of an old washing-up bottle and paint them the colour you want. To attach them to your fingers, paint your nails with clear nail varnish and carefully place the fake nails on your real ones. Allow the polish to dry and the nails will stick. Don't forget to ask your mother or sister first if you can borrow the nail varnish!

☐ To give yourself a beautiful bug-eyed look, carefully cut a table tennis ball in half and make holes at opposite sides of each half. Push a pin through each ball to create an eye-hole. Tie a length of elastic to the balls as shown, so that the bug-eyed goggles fit comfortably round your head.

Now use a felt-tipped pen or paints to draw a pupil on the front of each half ball, the more weirdly coloured the better.

☐ You can use half a table tennis ball to make yourself look like a Cyclops, sticking it to your forehead with plasticine. For added realism, wrap a bandage around your head so that only your Cyclops eye sticks out.

☐ Now go for it, Ugly Features!

● **MONSTER TIP**
To make ghostly faces, stand in front of a mirror in a darkened room, with a torch held just under your chin and shining up on to your face.

● **MONSTER TIP**
If you bend your index finger down on itself, you will be able to press the joint against your nostril and look as if you've managed to get your finger right up your nose. Ugh!

Mammothematics

Teachers: Q. Boyd, Algy Brah and Adam Upp

Monster School pupil: My pet vampire can do arithmetic.
Algy Brah: How?
Monster School pupil: Yesterday I asked him what three minus three was and he said nothing.

Monster School pupil: Sir, why do you call me 'wonder boy'?
Q. Boyd: Because I look at you and wonder.

Monster School pupil: What do you get when you cross a maths teacher with an alligator?
Adam Upp: Snappy answers.

Monster School Maths Lesson 1

Did you know that you go to school for only three whole days a year? This is how to prove it – it will drive your maths teacher crazy!

You sleep 8 hours a day, and $8 \times 365 = 2{,}920$ hours, which	= 122 days per year
You have 3 meals a day, and spend about an hour at each. $3 \times 365 = 1{,}095$ hours	= 46 days per year
You watch TV for about an hour a day which = 365 hours	= 15 days
There are 52 weekends in the year	= 104 days
School holidays account for about	75 days
TOTAL	= 362 days per year

And as there are 365 days in the year, there are only three days left for school!

Monster School Maths Lesson 2

Here are two sums that will also drive your maths teacher absolutely bananas.

● How to prove that $1 = 2$

Let us assume that $x = y$.
If this is the case, then $x - y$ must equal 0.
And so $2x - 2y$ must also equal 0.
But if both these sums come to 0, it must mean that $2x - 2y = x - y$.
Another way of saying this is: $2(x - y) = (x - y)$.
And if we divide each side of the equation by $(x - y)$ we get: $2 = 1$!

● How to prove that $1 = 0$

Let $x = 1$
Now multiply each side of the equation by x and you get $x^2 = x$.
Take away one from each side and you get:
$x^2 - 1 = x - 1$.
Another way of saying this is: $(x + 1)(x - 1) = (x - 1)$.
And if you divide each side by $x - 1$ you get: $x + 1 = 1$.
Take one away from each side and you're left with:
$x = 0$.
But right at the beginning we said that $x = 1$. So we have proved that $1 = 0$!

● **MONSTER TIP**

A good way to get your friends or enemies to faint is to show them the big nail that you've got sticking through your finger . . .

To make this trick, you will need a real nail that you've asked a grown-up to bend for you. Don't try to bend it yourself – you'll end up hurting yourself. When the nail has the correct bend in it, all you have to do is slip it over your finger and bingo! – instant injury. For added monstrosity, put a little tomato sauce on your finger as well, or put a plaster on with the nail sticking through it.

Monster School Jokes

As a monster pupil, you will always need to have a joke or two up your snotty sleeve ready for instant use.

Sometimes, for example, you will need to make a bully laugh so he doesn't notice that you're putting a bowl of hot custard down his trousers.

Sometimes you'll need to keep a teacher in hysterical fits of chuckling and chortling while you retrieve your exercise book from her desk, change all your answers, and get back to your own desk before she realizes what's going on.

But most of all, a joke (or ten) will come in handy just before you hand over your school report to your parents . . .

Monster teacher: Why are you so late?
Monster pupil: Sorry, miss, I overslept.
Monster teacher: You mean you sleep at home as well?

Monster teacher: You missed school yesterday, didn't you?
Monster pupil: Yes, sir – next time I'll try to improve my aim.

Monster teacher: You missed school yesterday, didn't you?
Monster pupil: No, sir, not a bit.

Monster teacher: What will you be when you leave school?
Monster pupil: Happy.

Monster headmaster: This is the fifth time this week that you've been sent to me for punishment. What have you to say for yourself?
Monster pupil: Thank goodness it's Friday!

Monster teacher on pupil's first day: And what might your name be?
Monster pupil: It might be Sebastian – but it isn't.

Monster pupil: Dad, I've been asked to leave Monster School.
Dad: For what?
Monster pupil: For good!

Monster teacher: Is that a sweet you're eating, boy?
Monster pupil: No, sir, it's a gumboil.
Monster teacher: Well, wait until playtime and then hand them round.

1st monster pupil: How many monster teachers work at Monster School?
2nd monster pupil: About half of them.

Monster teacher: Why do you keep on referring to Monster School as the blood bank?
Monster pupil: Because it's full of clots.

Monster teacher: Jason, stop trying to run the class. Do you think you're the monster teacher?

Monster pupil: No, sir.

Monster teacher: Then stop behaving like an idiot.

Monster teacher: Your son will definitely go down in history . . .

Monster mother: Oh?

Monster teacher: Yes, and in geography, and in French, and in maths . . .

● **MONSTER TIP**

Would you like to turn yourself into a ghost? Get someone to take a photograph of you standing on a staircase or in some other typically ghostly situation. Then, as soon as the photograph has been taken, move out of the way and get the person to take another picture without winding the film on and without moving the camera. When the film is developed, there will be a picture of you – but people will be able to see right through you!

Aaarrght! Class

Teachers: Stew D. Yeo and Di A. Gram

Monster School pupil: Look, sir. I've just painted your portrait. Don't you think it looks like you?
Stew D. Yeo: Er . . . well . . . it probably looks better from a distance.
Monster School pupil: I said it was like you.

Monster School pupil: Our art teacher is always complaining, so we call her the Mona Lisa.

Di. A. Gram: What are you making?
Monster School pupil: A portable.
Di. A. Gram: A portable what?
Monster School pupil: I don't know yet, so far I've only made the handle.

Monster Mugs

All these famous monsters were once pupils at the Monster School. Can you identify them?

2.

5.

3.

What's This?

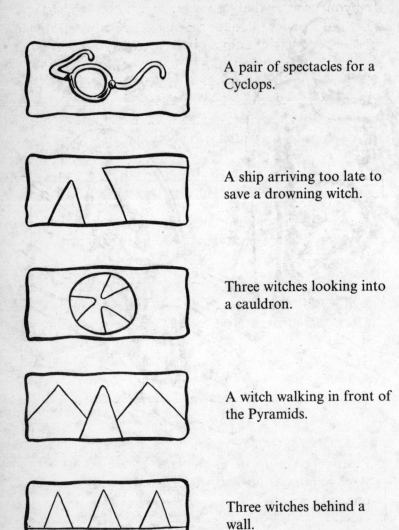

A pair of spectacles for a Cyclops.

A ship arriving too late to save a drowning witch.

Three witches looking into a cauldron.

A witch walking in front of the Pyramids.

Three witches behind a wall.

A Monster Trick to Play on Aaarrght! Teachers

Tell your teacher that you want to sell him (or her) a beautiful copper plaque bearing a portrait of the Queen, exquisitely sculpted in bas relief (your teacher will know what you mean by this, even if you don't). All you want for this genuine work of art, you say, is ten pence . . .

When your teacher hands over the money, you present him or her with a two pence piece!

- **MONSTER TIP**

Make a *papier mâché* head that looks as much like you as possible and carry it under your arm.

- **MONSTER TIP**

Borrow some very large clothes from one of your parents and try to get into them with a friend. With luck, you'll create a rather nice two-headed monster.

- **MONSTER TIP**

Put a big dollop of marmalade in the palm of your hand and go and shake hands with some-one.

Frightfully French

Teacher: M'sewer DuPong

M'sewer DuPong: Which monster was president of France for many years?
Monster School pupil: Charles de Ghoul.

Lesson 1: A Monster Vocabulary List to Drive Your French Teacher Crackers

In French	In Monster School English
Champagne	fake window
Entrechat	entry for the cat
Faux pas	an enemy of father
Non merci	no mercy
S'il vous plaît	silver plate
Entrez	on the tray
Coup de grâce	cut the grass
Pas du tout	father of two
Défense d'afficher	defend the fishes
Je ne comprends pas	I do not understand father
Hors de combat	horse of combat
Moi aussi	I am an Australian

Lesson 2: A Monster French Poem in English

The French monster saw in the hall
A pool that some fool had let fall;
He said: 'Ah, oui, oui!
This time it's not me,
But I'm bound to be blamed for it all.'

Et maintenant, *A Monster French Poem in French – or is it?*

This poem is guaranteed to turn your teacher's hair grey overnight – unless it's already grey, in which case it will turn purple, with green tufts and orange dandruff. Set the joke up by telling your teacher that you found the poem in a book of ancient French poetry, and that the authors believed the text to be at least three hundred years old and possibly in a strange dialect. Your teacher will study the poem for ages (if you're lucky, for another three hundred years) before finally admitting that the translation is impossible.

That's when you step forward and recite the poem in English . . . because the poem is actually nothing more complicated than Humpty Dumpty, written phonetically!

Homme petit, d'hommes petits,
C'est on d'y ou Arles.
Homme petit, d'hommes petits,
A des Griffes Orles.
Alte quinze Or cesses,
Anne d'Arles de quinze Ermennes,
Qu'on de ne Poute
Homme petit tu guer d'Agen.

If your teacher has any energy (or sanity!) left, try him or her with this one:

Pas deux leur Rhone que nous.

Again, it's phonetic, and it says: Paddle her own canoe!

● MONSTER TIP
How to keep the school genius happy. On one side of a sheet of paper, write: THE STATEMENT ON THE OTHER SIDE OF THIS PAPER IS FALSE. On the other side of the sheet, write: THE STATEMENT ON THE OTHER SIDE OF THIS PAPER IS TRUE.

---

20 Monster Things to Do When There's Nothing to Do

Let's face it, even the biggest monster knows that there are times of the day when there's nobody around to be pestered or terrified, and that's when good monsters use all their cunning, skill and ingenuity to stop themselves from getting bored. Here are a few examples to get you going, but you can probably think of loads more:

1. Get down on your hands and knees and growl at the carpet.

2. Go outside and call: 'Dracula, here boy! Come and get your litre of blood for din-dins!'

3. Write down the names of ten different monsters.

4. Try to find them in the phone book.

5. Pull different monster faces in the mirror until you scare yourself.

6. Try to get both feet into the same sock to turn yourself into a one-footed monster.

7. Try to touch your nose with your tongue, or your tongue with your nose – whichever is easier.

8. When you succeed, take a photograph of yourself doing it and send it to *Monster News*.

9. If it's snowing outside, stand in a carrier bag and hop around making huge Yeti-type footprints that terrify the neighbourhood.

10. Then, still in the carrier bag, pick yourself up by the handles until you levitate like a phantom.

11. Try to work out why it didn't work.

12. If you're a werewolf, wash all your hair – one at a time.

13. Find an old magazine and add monster features to all the pictures.

14. Check your pulse. If you have one, bad luck – it means you're not a Zombie.

15. Think of how big the universe is and how many monsters there must be out there in space.

16. Try to become The Abominable Underpant Monster – see how many pairs of underpants you can put on on top of each other.

17. Count all the times the word **monster** appears in this book.

18. Are you sure? Count them again.

19. Peel an orange with your toes.

20. Examine the palms of your hands and see if there are any hairs on them.

● **MONSTER TIP**

Want to know what a dead finger feels like? With your right hand clasp someone's left hand so that your index fingers are extended and touching along their whole length. Now ask your friend to use the finger and thumb of their other hand to feel the index fingers. As your friend moves their hand up and down, with their thumb touching their own finger and their index finger touching yours, your friend will receive a strange sensation of numbness, as if he or she has lost some feeling in that finger.

Domestic Seance (Spookery)

Teacher: Victoria Sponge

Monster School pupil: I don't like my granny.
Victoria Sponge: Have you tried her with salt and pepper?

Monster School pupil: What are we cooking for lunch today?
Victoria Sponge: Shut up and get back in the oven.

Monster child: Mummy, Mummy, can I bring a friend home for tea?
Monster mother: Of course, dear – put him in the fridge and we'll have him later.

Victoria Sponge: Why did the female monster go on a diet?
Monster School pupil: To keep her ghoulish figure.

Victoria Sponge: What do monsters eat for breakfast?
Monster School pupil: Dreaded Wheat.

Victoria Sponge: How do you make a monster stew?
Monster School pupil: Keep it waiting for two hours.

Victoria Sponge: How do ghosts eat food?
Monster School pupil: By goblin it.

Lesson 1

We expect all our pupils to come to the Monster School already knowing how to burn toast, scramble a teacher's brains and make an absolutely perfect upside-down kitchen. So in Lesson 1, it's time for you to put all your skills into practice. Nothing too grand or ambitious to start with. Just that all-time classic favourite of monster cuisine:

Crispy Maggots in Chocolate Sauce

Ingredients
1 kilo of fresh writhing maggots
1 tin of dogfood
3 bars of chocolate
$\frac{1}{2}$ kilo of worms, freshly squashed
100 grams of butter or old engine oil
200 grams of sugar or crispy fried lice
1 tube toothpaste

Soak the maggots thoroughly in old dishwater until they stop wriggling and float to the surface.

Heat the old engine oil in a frying pan, and fry the maggots until golden brown.

Melt the chocolate, add the remaining ingredients and stir well.

Add the maggots to this mixture, pour the chocolate sauce over it, and place in the fridge until set.

Serve cold with whipped toothpaste and run like the clappers.

Lesson 2

Next week, how to make butterfly cakes with real butterflies, shepherd's pie with real shepherds, cottage pie with real cottages and Victoria sponge with real Victorias . . .

● **MONSTER TIP**
Take a piece of orange peel, about a quarter of an orange, and cut it into fangs. Wedge one piece under your top lip, and the other under your bottom lip so that they cover your own teeth. Now start snarling!

● **MONSTER TIP**
Chew a raisin a bit until it looks squashy and horrible. Place it in your hand and go up to a friend. Pretend that there is a fly in the room, and pretend to grab it in your hand. Open up your hand and pull off the squashed raisin. Now start eating it!

Monsterology

Here are some details on just about every monster known. As you read the descriptions, try to work out whom in your class each monster most closely resembles ... (Don't forget to include your family and teachers as well!)

● **Vampires** leave their graves at night and suck human blood. They need fresh blood to survive, so their victims are always living people or corpses of people who have just died.

The Vampire I know is called..

● **Gorgons** were horrible monsters that looked like ugly old women with hair made of live snakes. Anyone who looked at a Gorgon instantly turned to stone.

The Gorgon I know is called ....

The Banshee is a Gaelic spirit whose wail warns of approaching death.

The Banshee I know is called ....

● The female equivalent of a **werewolf** is called an **Estrie**. She can change her shape at will and drinks children's blood. When an Estrie dies her mouth is filled with earth to prevent her from doing evil again.

The Werewolf I know is called ....

The Estrie I know is called ....

● The most horrifying of Irish monsters is the **Fachan**, which has just one large eye in the middle of its forehead and a ghastly, scaly body. It feeds on the flesh of people who travel late at night.

The Fachan I know is called ....

● Some monsters are plants! In his book *The Day of the Triffids*, John Wyndham created huge plants called **triffids** which could roam the countryside and sting people to death.

The closest person in my class to a Triffid is ....

● In Greek mythology, the **Minotaur** was a monster that was half man and half bull, and that ate seven boys and seven girls each year. The Minotaur lived in a maze, and if you got into it by mistake you'd never escape.

The Minotaur I know is called ....

• The **Abominable Snowman** or **Yeti** has been sighted on many occasions by mountaineers. It leaves gigantic footprints in the snow – bigger than those of any living animal.

The Yeti I know is called...

• **Count Dracula** really did exist. His real name was Prince Vlad Dracula, and he became known as Vlad the Impaler because he used to impale his victims on wooden stakes to make sure they died a slow, horrible death. He then cooked their bodies and fed them to their unsuspecting families.

The Dracula I know is called..

• A monster called **Afanc**, half horse and half man, is believed to live in mountain pools in Wales and to be almost impossible to kill.

The Afanc I know is called...

• **Zombies** are monsters that look like living people – and indeed they were alive once – but now they are the walking dead. Zombies' faces are drained of blood and their eyes have a terrifying stare and never blink. They never speak, and never seem to breathe.

The Zombie I know is called ....

• The lowlands of Scotland are the home of the **Nuckelavee**, a monster that looks like a skinless old man with a huge ugly head, no legs and very long arms. He has terrible breath that kills any plant that he breathes on.

The Nuckelavee I know is called ....

● Another famous Scottish monster is the **Boobrie**, which looks like an enormous duck. It feeds on sheep and cows, which it can take in one mouthful.

The Boobrie I know is called ....

• A fire-spitting monster called the **Chimera** lived in Asia Minor and killed anyone who tried to attack it. The Chimera had the head of a lion, the body of a goat and the tail of a dragon.

The Chimera I know is called..

• In 1512 a beast was born which came to be known as the **Monster of Ravenna**. It had a human body, but there was a horn on its head, and it had two wings, one foot (with claws), and only one kneecap – in which there was an eye.

The Monster of Ravenna I know is called.....................

• In Greek mythology, the Gorgons were said to be protected by three monsters called the **Graeae**, who were horrible even in hell. The Graeae were grey in colour and had only one eye and one tooth between them, which they passed from one to another.

The three Graeae I know are called.............................
....

• In Norway and other Scandinavian countries there are many legends about **Trolls**, who are ugly, hump-back dwarfs with long crooked noses. They are said to steal human babies and substitute them for their own, but you are safe from such attacks if you stay in the sunshine: the sun's rays turn Trolls into stone.

The Troll I know is called ....

• In Ancient Egypt, **Anubis**, the god of the dead, was believed to weigh the heart of every dead person in the underworld. If it did not balance with the feather of truth in the opposite scale it was eaten by **Ammit**, a horrible monster – half lion, half hippopotamus, with the jaws of a crocodile.

The Anubis I know is called ....

The Ammit I know is called ....

• A giant monster called **Kraken** is believed to roam the coast of Norway. Like a monstrous squid, it has tentacle-like arms over ten metres long, is bigger than a ship and colours the water black so that it can hide beneath the murky surface.

The Kraken I know is called..

• A monster called **Lamia** is half woman and half serpent, and eats every child she comes across.

The Lamia I know is called ....

• The most elusive monster of all is the **Loch Ness Monster,** which is believed to have a snake-like head and a body that is twelve metres long. Nessie has been sighted many times, and with Loch Ness having a depth of 230 metres, scientists say that it is quite possible that a monster could live down there.

The Loch Ness Monster I know is called ....

Hysterical History

Teacher: Holden Days

Holden Days: Where were the kings and queens of England crowned?
Monster School pupil: On their heads.

Holden Days: Did you know that Columbus found America?
Monster School pupil: I didn't even know it was lost.

Holden Days: How long was Elizabeth the First on the throne?
Monster School pupil: The same length as she was off it.

Monster School History Lesson

First there was the Ice Age, then the Stone Age, then the Bronze Age. Next came the Saus Age.

Some English monarchs were Henry VII, Henry VIII, Edward VI and Mary. Who came after Mary? Why, the lamb of course!

The first thing Edward II did on coming to the throne was to sit down.

King John signed the Magna Carta at the bottom.

When Sir Walter Raleigh dropped his cloak in front of Queen Elizabeth I, he said, 'Step on it, kid.'

What were some Poles doing in England in 1940? Holding up the telephone wires.

● MONSTER TIP

Create a ghostly tapping sound by tying a button to a piece of cotton thread and hanging it outside a bedroom window. When the wind blows during the night there will be a scary, monstrous tap, tap, tap sound at the window.

Monster Quips for the Canteen Queue

Guaranteed to Delight the Dinner Ladies!

'This fly looks extremely well cooked.'

'Did you kill this cabbage yourself?'

'The sauce looks very artistic – just like paint.'

'Do you have any indigestion tablets for dessert?'

'What kind of eggs are these – pterodactyl's?'

'May I have another plate for the maggots?'

'I know the fish fingers are dead, but there's no need to cremate them.'

'Are those sultanas, or do you keep rabbits under the counter?'

'Are these sesame seeds, or have you been picking your nose?'

● **MONSTER TIP**
Sit in a room full of people and start scratching yourself as if a flea is running around all over you.

MONSTER
SCHOOL
~~MENU~~ Poison list

AVAILABLE NOW IN THE ~~CANTEEN~~ execution chamber

MAIN COURSES

Sausages & mash ← Doggy do and cotton wool

Egg & chips ← eyeballs + soggy dead men's fingers

Beef burgers & chips fried beermats + dead slugs in vaseline

Macaroni cheese ← drainpipes in polyfilla

Tomato juice ← vampire blood

Spaghetti bolognaise = worms in sewage

Sandwiches

Mashed banana squashed rat

Pâté & lettuce ← old clay + stinging nettles

Peanut butter & jam ← nutshells + blood clots

cream cheese & chives ↷ custard + bogeys

Prawn cocktail . ← worms in washing up detergent

Bacon & lettuce dog food with seaweed

Cottage cheese & apple toothpaste with gravel

Roast beef with coleslaw hamster bedding + vomit

Salad with mayonnaise . hedge clippings + cat sick

Sweets

Chocolate custard ↶ radioactive effluent

Tapioca ← frog spawn

Plums & custard ← conkers in slug slime

Jam tart ← crusty old bandages

Treacle tart ← tarmac path

Cheese & biscuits ↑ Soap + cardboard

Or for a much tastier meal, eat this menu !!

Geography

Teachers: Coral Reefe and Farah Way

Coral Reefe: How can you prove the world is round?
Monster School pupil: I never said it was.

Farah Way: What is a Laplander?
Monster School pupil: Someone who falls over on a bus.

Farah Way: What is your favourite country?
Monster School pupil: Mozambique.
Farah Way: Spell it.
Monster School pupil: On second thoughts, I think I prefer Italy.

Monster School Geography Lesson 1

People who live in Delhi are called Dahlias.
People who live in Moscow are called Mosques.
People who live in Naples are called Napoleons.
People who live in Fiji are called Fidgets.
People who live in Sardinia are called Sardines.
People who live in Hamburg are called Hamburgers.

Monster School Geography Lesson 2

The Andes are at the end of the armies.

Eskimos use iced lolly.

The language they speak in Cuba is Cubic.

The small rivers that flow into the Nile are called Juveniles.

The wettest place in Britain is Bath.

The Statue of Liberty stands in New York harbour because it can't sit down.

Felixstowe is at the end of Felix's foot.

Timbuktu is somewhere between Timbuck-one and Timbuk-three.

The highest mountain in the world before Mount Everest was discovered was Mount Everest.

Monster School News

This week's cover ghoul is the lovely Paula Face from 5C

Make-up by Chris Lee Bare (4A)
Hair by Spike E. Hairdo (3B)
Clothes by U. R. Ugly (5A)

Inside This Week's Issue:

Are your bogeys past their sell-by date?
Our nose-picking expert tells you how to keep them fresh and slimy!

Your horror-scope
What the future holds for Hairies.

How to be greener and smellier with rancid yellow teeth. *Plus!* Pollution – how to cause it.

Dress to depress!
Bags of advice on the latest ugly fashions.

Grow a hairy chest
Our ugly expert tells you how. And for the boys – how to make your spots bigger and attract more girls . . .

Plus!
Build a cupboard for your ear-wax collection!
And much, much more!

Party Studies: How to Have a Monster Mash!

Once a year, there is a very special day in the calendar that every monster wants to celebrate – its burpday. But it takes a lot of thought and planning to make sure a party goes with a swing – and thought and planning are two things that don't come naturally to monsters! No wonder Party Studies is such an important subject in the Monster School Curriculum.

Lesson 1: The Menu

A Few Favourites That Always Go Down Well:

- Fish fungus with pickled bunions
- Baked beings on toast
- Eyes cream with fresh blood ripple

- Meat-eating monsters might enjoy a nice plateful of barbecued vicar, but beware of giving them too much: it's hard to keep a good man down.

- If your guests are vegetarians, on the other hand, try giving them boiled Swedes. Or, if you want to be really fancy, try roasted Norwegians or casseroled Danes.

- To make a tasty Gorgon's head for dessert, use a melon as the head and decorate it with pieces of fruit to make a mouth, eyes and nose. The hair can be liquorice laces from the sweet shop.

Lesson 2: Fun and Games

Every monster should know how to have monster fun – and that means playing monster games like Blind Monster's Bluff, Ten Green Monsters, Musical Monsters, card games like Snap (with real crocodiles), and gentle little nursery rhyme games for tiddly-widdly toddler monsters, like Wring-a Wring-a Nosie. Here are a few other suggestions to keep you amused:

- **What's the Time, Mr Werewolf?**
- **Stick the Stake in the Vampire's Heart**
- **Pass the Pimple**
- **Swallow My Leader**
- **Haunt and Seek**

And here are some more complicated games, that need a bit of explanation:

Hunt the Witch's Magic Charm

Thread a ring (a curtain ring will do) on to a long length of string and tie the two ends of string together.

One player is chosen to be the witchhunter and stands in the middle of the circle of string. The other players stand around him or her in a circle, with their two hands gripped over the string. They must try to move the magic charm around the string from person to person without it being spotted.

The Ghost of the Cave

This is a really monstrous game, especially if you play it in the dark. In a monstery voice that is scary enough to chill the bravest blood, you say to your friend: 'I am the ghost of the cave, and I'm coming to haunt you tonight ... Sally ... Sally ... I'm on your one step ...'

(Make your voice even more monstrous:)

'Sally, I'm on your two step ...'

'Sally, I'm on your three step ...'

'Sally, I'm on your four step ...'

'Sally, I'm on your bedroom door ...'

'Sally, I'VE GOT YOU!!'

You can keep this game going for a long time, the point being to create an element of surprise so that your victim doesn't know when you are going to shout 'I'VE GOT YOU!'

Monster Who?

Write on a number of pieces of card the names of a number of monsters, and get each player to pick a card. Without showing the card to any other person, each player must draw his monster. When the drawing is complete, each player holds up his or her picture and the others have to guess the name of the monster.

Screamin' Demon!

Everybody sits in a circle and all the lights are put out so that the room is in total darkness. Now you start to tell the story of a particularly gruesome murder . . .

First, tell everyone that the murderer began by goug-ing out the victim's eyes, and pass round two freshly peeled grapes. Next, say that the murderer cut off the victim's ear, and pass around a suitable item – you can make a nice ear from the bottom part of a cab-bage leaf. Then the victim's brain can be a wet sponge, his fingers carrots, his teeth bits of broken macaroni, and so on and so on. If anyone screams or makes the slightest sound, they are out . . . and by the time you pass around a handful of crisps and say that they are the victim's scabs, everybody usually is!

Ghosts

This is a very simple – but funny – game. Two teams are formed, and one team leaves the room. The play-ers in this team then take it in turn to cover themselves with a white bedsheet and appear in front of the other team, wailing in a ghostly, monstrous way. The opposing team has to guess who is under the sheet each time. When everyone in the first team has ap-peared, the teams swap places. The team with the highest number of correct guesses wins.

Monster Consequences

Divide into teams of four (if possible). Each team has a sheet of paper and a pencil or pen. Divide the sheet of paper into four sections, and draw a monster's head on the top section. Then fold it over backwards, so that your drawing can't be seen. Pass it on to the next person, who must draw a body on the middle section. They then fold this section over as well, and the next person in the team draws a pair of legs on the bottom section. The last person must invent a name for the team's monster, and write it in the last section. Then each team opens up its sheet of paper and exposes its creation. The team with the most gruesome-looking monster is the winner.

Make a Monster

You need a dice and paper and pencil for each player. The aim is to be the first to complete the drawing of a monster, by throwing the correct number for each part. You take turns to throw, and cannot start until you throw a one for the body.

You need to throw: a one for the body, a two for the head, a three for each strand of hair (decide before the game starts how many strands each monster should have), a four for each arm or leg (decide beforehand how many arms and legs each monster needs), a five for each part of its face – mouth, nose, eyes (decide how many of each), a six for each ear.

You can't start drawing the face or ears until you have drawn the head, of course, and you can make your monster any shape – but you must have the agreed number of parts on its body.

Which Mummy?

This is a brilliant game, but do make sure that an adult monster has given you permission to play it!

Each pair of players needs a full toilet roll.

Each pair then decides who is going to be the Mummy and who is going to be the Wrapper-up. Set a time limit of, say, three minutes for the wrapping up.

On the command 'WRAP!' the wrappers must start to wrap up their mummies with the whole toilet roll so that they look as much like an Egyptian mummy as possible.

At the end of the time, see whose mummy is best.

Monster Noises

This is a great game for breaking the ice at parties. For each pair of players, write the name of a monster on two pieces of paper, fold them up, and put them in two different hats or boxes. A few examples are:

Ghost
Loch Ness Monster
King Kong
Frankenstein's Monster
Count Dracula
Werewolf
Banshee
Hound of the Baskervilles
Creature from the Black Lagoon
Witch

When your guests arrive, they each choose a piece of paper from one of the hats. On the word GO, they must then try to find their partner only by making the right noise for that particular monster!

Fearsome Feelies

For this game you need a large bowl of soapy water or a large covered basket or box, a pencil and paper for each player, and several objects with a different kind of feel – for example, a prune, a soft toy, a walnut, a piece of rope, a carrot.

Each player in turn must slip their hand into the bowl or basket (without removing the covering, of

course) and feel the objects without looking at them. Give each player just thirty seconds or so to feel around, and then, when they have finished, get them to list the objects. The player with the most correct list wins.

Another way of playing this game is to use some really horrible objects like a piece of soggy bread wrapped in cling-film, an over-ripe tomato, a used tea-bag and an uncooked sausage, and for each player to write down the most horrible thing that they think it feels like. The winner is the person with the most vivid and monstrous imagination: was the old tea-bag a piece of monkey's brain, for example, a squashed eye, a monster's toe or just a writhing mass of man-eating worms?

● MONSTER TIP

Scare your friends by telling them that you have a monster's head in a box. It is too terrifying to look at, you say, but if they want to they can feel it through a small hole in the box.

Inside the box you have put a melon with part of the top scooped out and filled with cold spaghetti. Use squishy grapes stuck to the melon with cocktail sticks for eyes, and something like a carrot for a nose. Cut out a slot for the mouth, and fill it with macaroni teeth.

Spurts (Fizzical Education)

Teachers: *Daley X. R. Size, Althea Lettix, Jim Nastix and Jim Shooze*

Jim Shooze: What games do ghost children play?
Monster School pupil: Haunt and seek.

Jim Nastix: What games do monster children play?
Monster School pupil: Hyde and sick.

Daley X. R. Size: What helps ghosts win games?
Monster School pupil: Their team spirit.

Jim Shooze: What is a vampire's favourite sport?
Monster School pupil: Skin diving.

Althea Lettix: What kind of horses do monsters use for racing?
Monster School pupil: Nightmares.

Jim Nastix: What is Count Dracula's favourite sport?
Monster School pupil: Bat-minton.

Monster Movie Guide

What is the best way to describe monster films? Spook-tacular!

This Week's Top 13 Monster Movies

The Abominable Dr Phibes
The Wasp Woman
The Wolf Man
Zombie Flesh Eaters
Attack of the Puppet People
The Beast from 20,000 Fathoms
The Beast in the Cellar
Blood from the Mummy's Tomb
The Cars that Ate Paris
The Giant Spider Invasion
The House that Dripped Blood
The Savage Bees
The Things with Two Heads

Monster Movie Facts

● Alfred Hitchcock, director of the greatest suspense movies, was born on Friday the 13th.

● In a 1962 film a monster called **Reptilicus** was dug up in Denmark. Once in the laboratory, the prehistoric lizard comes alive again and starts to destroy everything in sight.

• In a 1963 horror film called ***The Slime People***, disgusting prehistoric blobs of slime attempt to take over the world.

• The star of a truly ghastly horror film was called ***The Crawling Eye***. It was a large eye that crawled along the ground on its own, propelled by tentacles and letting out a poisonous gas.

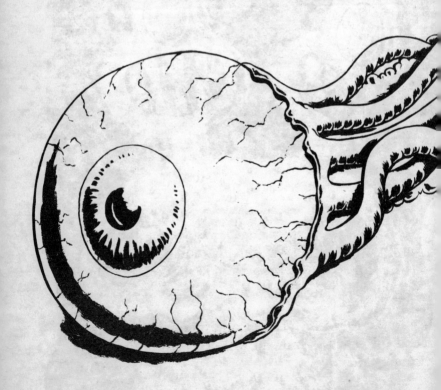

● The *Creature from the Black Lagoon* was the horrifying monster in a 1954 film. A cross between a man and a frog, this ugly brute lived in the Amazon jungle, deep in the mud.

● In the 1958 film *The Fly*, an experiment goes wrong and the scientist ends up with a fly's head instead of his own.

• The most famous screen Count Dracula was Bela Lugosi, who was so ugly that he needed very little make-up. When he died in 1956, he was buried in the black cape with a red satin lining which he had worn in all his Dracula films.

• A fire-breathing monster called *Ghidrah* was created for a film in Japan. It had three heads and was indestructible.

• In all the films and books about Frankenstein's monster, nobody has ever managed to kill him. So he must still be out there somewhere . . .

• **MONSTER TIP**
Cut out different eyes, ears, noses, mouths, hairstyles, arms, legs and bodies from old newspapers and magazines and mix them up to create new, monstrous people.

Monster School Music Lesson

Teachers: *P. Ann O'Forty and Vi O'Lynn*

There was a young monster called Green,
Whose musical sense wasn't keen;
He said: 'It is odd,
But I cannot tell "God
Save the Weasel" from "Pop Goes the Queen"!'

A tutor who taught monsters flute
Tried to teach two young tooters to toot:
Said the two to the tutor:
'Is it harder to toot, or
To tutor two tooters to toot?'

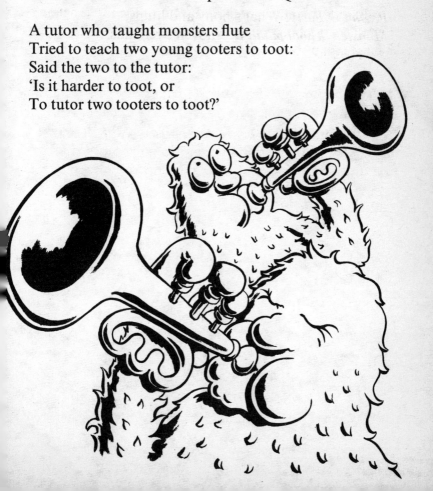

Vi O'Lynn: What is your favourite instrument?
Monster School pupil: The dinner bell.

P. Ann O'Forty: I'd like to be able to play the cornet.
Monster School pupil: I'd rather lick it.

Vi O'Lynn: Is there anything special you'd like to play?
Monster School pupil: Yes, miss – truant.

P. Ann O'Forty: What's bony and hums?
Monster School pupil: Beethoven's remains.

The Problem Page

Do you have too few spots? Does your face look too human? Do you wish you had three heads and ten nostrils?

Write to Ivor Wartybum. Ivor is the Monster School's leading expert on wart transplants, bum goils (sorry – gum boils), werewolf baldness, and fang decay.

Dear Ivor

Yes, I have a problem. I am a vampire but I faint at the sight of blood. What should I do?

Pearce Nex (4A)

● *Dear Pearce*

Become a vegetarian. But whatever you do, steer clear of blood oranges – and necktarines!

Dear Ivor

Last night at the Monster School Disco, a fabulously ugly girl rolled her eyes at me. What shall I do?

Globule Fat-Bogey (3B)

● *Dear Globule*

Roll them back, you fool – she might need them.

Dear Ivor

I am the Head Boy at the Monster School and last term I met the girl of my dreams and completely lost my head. Now I'm the Headless Boy and my girlfriend says she finds it very hard to kiss me because my face has gone. Any suggestions?

Mr X of 5C

• *Dear Mr X*

If you'd lost your tail it would have been easier. I would have just told you to go to a retail shop. But you could always try going to a headhunter. If that doesn't work, give your girlfriend my phone number.

Dear Ivor

When I was ten years old I started growing hair all over my body. I asked my mother if I was a werewolf, but all she said was, 'Shut up and keep combing your face.' Then the doctor told me that I was indeed a werewolf, and I was over the moon. I was so hairy and ugly you wouldn't believe it, and all the boys loved me. But just recently my hair has started to fall out. What can I use to keep it in?

Tracey Vicious (1B)

• *Dear Tracey*

Try a cardboard box.

Dear Ivor

My problem is that I hate going to Monster School and I'd much rather stay at home all day, filling in my colouring books and watching *Sesame Street*. Every morning when I wake up I pretend to be ill, but my mummy never believes me and never lets me stay at home with her. All the way to the bus I try to think of excuses for not going, because I know that the teachers are going to make fun of me all day and the children are going to tease me. Please, please, please help me and tell me what to do!

Reginald Gunge-Bucket

● *Dear Reginald*
I'm sorry, but you really must go to school every day. After all, you are *the headmaster!*

National Curriculum: Monster School Pupil Assessment

Name of pupil ....

Social skills I won't say she's unpopular, but everyone calls her 'Laryngitis' because she's such a pain in the neck.

Contribution to school life She is about as useful as a chocolate teapot.

Ability to concentrate We presume her tiny brain is on permanent holiday.

Physical ability I think she was born upside down. Her nose runs and her feet smell.

General intelligence There's nothing wrong with her brain. Nothing that a transplant wouldn't cure.

Reasoning ability There is more brainpower in a Zombie's toenail.

Musical ability The only thing she can play is her Walkman.

Geography She's the only pupil I know who thinks the Andes are things that you find on the end of your wristies.

Anguish Language She has a great flair for creative writing. Another way of saying that is that she's a liar.

Hiss-tory She has a very good head for dates. Maybe that's because her face looks like a date.

Mammothematics She has average ability for her group. Mind you, the rest of the group are in the gorilla cage at London Zoo.

Fizzical Education She has represented the school in all team sports. (There are only eleven girls in the school.)

Woodwork She has produced a great deal of work this term – six bags of sawdust.

Aaarrgght! She has really immersed herself in this subject – but don't worry, the paint will eventually come off.

National Curriculum: Monster School Pupil Assessment

Name of pupil ....

Social skills This student's presence has lit up the classroom. He set fire to it.

Contribution to school life He has made his mark on the school, and I've made a few on him.

Ability to concentrate His mind often wanders but we don't worry – it's too weak to go very far.

Physical ability He has muscles in his arms like potatoes – mashed potatoes.

General intelligence He's much cleverer than he looks, but then I suppose he'd have to be.

Reasoning ability He stinks, therefore he is.

Musical ability He has a good singing voice – if you don't happen to like music. On the violin this term, he played Mozart. Mozart lost.

Geography Couldn't find his way out of a paper bag.

Anguish Language His spelling presents no problems, but that's probably because we can't read his writing.

Hiss-tory He has expressed quite an interest in this subject. Well, he asked where he should have been yesterday.

Mammothematics Advanced maths does cause him some problems: he has to take his shoes off to count higher than 10.

Fizzical Education Is very useful in team games, mainly because we use him as a goal post.

Woodwork He has great ability in this subject, but then he would, wouldn't he, being as thick as a plank.

Aaarrgght! Has made great progress this term. He can now hold a pencil with the pointed end downwards.

So you think you have learnt everything that Monster School can teach you, do you – and you reckon you're ready to sit for your GCSE in Antisocial Studies? Well, OK, smarty-pants, here's where we find out . . .

The Monster School Exams

Dip your claws in the bloodpot, and get writing . . .

(NB: Pupils must scribble and dribble on one side of the paper only.)

Examination rule: Anyone found cheating will be awarded ten marks for initiative.

1. What was the main diet of the *Zombie Flesh Eaters*?

2. And of *The Cars That Ate Paris*?

3. There have been four movies called *Nightmare on Elm Street*. The first three were called *Nightmare on Elm Street*, *Nightmare on Elm Street II*, and *Nightmare on Elm Street III*. Name the fourth one.

4. Approximately how deep in the ocean was *The Beast from 20,000 Fathoms*?

5. Who won the *War of the Worlds*?

6. Who came second?

7. Who built Frankenstein's Monster? Was it (a) McAlpines, (b) Wimpeys, (c) Taylor Woodrow, or (d) someone else?

8. What does the smell of fresh blood look like?

9. Either construct a living, breathing monster from a bag of frozen chicken legs, a pig's head, a lamb's liver and 15,000 volts of electricity, or write your name in block capitals.

10. Queen Boadicea's favourite horse was called *The Abominable Dr Phibes*. True or false?

Do Horses have to take their hay levels?

In every exam I nearly got 100% — Well, I got the two noughts anyway

Go to school to learn the three R's — ravage, riot and revolution

Do gardeners study for
a dig-ree?

Did Father
Christmas have to
take his ho-ho-ho levels?

If you are not confused
you have misunderstood
the question

Avoid the rush -
fail your exams now

tip for
Oral exams:
if in doubt,
mumble.

Leaving School: Monster Careers Advice

Even at Monster School, there comes a day (sob, sob) when you have to clear all the dead rats and festering gumboils out of your desk, shake your teachers by the hand (make sure to leave them with a good squelch of gooey bogies between their fingers), and wend your merry, monstrous way into the outside world as you crash through the school gates for the very last time.

But what do you do next? There's only one university in the country that offers a course that would interest you, and that's the degree in Applied Monstrosity at the University of Wails.

And if it's an ordinary job that you're looking for, you'll find there isn't much call for professional monsters down at the Job Centre – so you might have to re-train. Here are a few good jobs you could try:

- An astronaut's job is really out of this world.
- If you want to be a flea trainer when you leave school, you'll have to be prepared to start from scratch.
- If you want to be a roaring success, become a lion tamer.
- An oil driller's work is boring.
- To be a lumberjack you have to be a decent feller.
- If you want to go up in the world, try being a lift operator.
- For a job you can stick to, become a glue maker.

- If you become a baker you'll always make plenty of dough.
- If your teachers have always been telling you you're a drop-out, you might be successful as a parachutist.
- Of course, you could always become a human cannonball – but you must be a person of the right calibre, and willing to travel.

And if none of these appeal to you, why not become a chimney sweep – that should soot you.